The 5 Minute Discipleship Journal

A simple, yet powerful tool to help you
grow daily as a disciple of Jesus.

CREATED BY
LOREN HICKS

Dedicated to those who want a deeper, more intimate relationship with Jesus
Christ.

Published by 5 Minute Discipleship
5MinuteDiscipleship.com

Printed in the United States of America

First Edition

Introduction

For as long as I can remember, I have heard about the necessity of a daily devotional time with God. It makes sense, right? You cannot have a relationship with someone unless you spend time with them. But how do we spend time with God? Is there a right structure or process? Of course, we know we should read the Bible and pray, but is that all there is to it? Do we check a box signing off on our daily Christian duty? Or is there more?

For most of us, having a guide is helpful. If you are hiking in unfamiliar territory, a guide makes sure you do not get lost and that you see and experience everything you need for a great experience. This book is a 90-day guide. It provides enough space for you to track your devotional time for three months. Step by step, you will discover how your quiet time with Jesus can be something rich and meaningful. I have included prompts and accountability into the journal to help you find the consistency you desire.

In August of 2020, during the Covid-19 shutdown, I started a daily podcast called *The 5 Minute Discipleship Podcast*. My goal is to inspire people like you towards a deeper, more intimate relationship with Christ. This book is a complement to the podcast. You can use this book to follow along with the podcast and journal how God is speaking to you. Or, you can select your own daily scripture reading and reflection.

I have found journaling to be an effective spiritual discipline for the following reasons.

1. It forces me to slow down - It takes time to write. The discipline has been helpful because if I am not careful, it is easy to speed through my quiet time and move on to other things.

2. It facilitates meditation on the scripture and makes me process my thoughts - Journaling causes me to engage with the scripture, to ask questions, and to look for points of application. If I am just reading the Bible, I do not always do this.

3. I tend to remember things I write down - There is an old saying that I believe is true: "the shortest pencil is longer than the longest memory."

4. It gives me a record of what God is doing in my life. It is rewarding to read what God was saying to me a year ago.

5. I am more engaged, and it is harder for my mind to wander. We all know what it is like to begin praying or reading the Bible and have our minds wander to other things. Journaling helps me focus my thoughts on the Word of God.

As I put this journal together, I have prayed for you. I am asking God to speak to your heart and life and that you will put into practice what He says. I believe the results will be life-changing.

I would love to hear how the journal is helping your grow as a follower of Jesus. You can email me at loren@5minutediscipleship.com

Let the journey begin!

Loren Hicks

Claim Your Free Bonuses

To provide as much value to you as possible, I put together an exclusive bonus package for *The 5 Minute Discipleship Journal* users.

1. A Digital Version of *The 5 Minute Discipleship Journal*

Some readers requested a digital version of the journal to use with their tablet and stylus. I'm happy to provide this to you for free.

2. Reignite Your Spiritual Passion

This is a free, seven-day email course I designed for those who are wanting spiritual renewal. If you are running on empty and want to restart your spiritual life, I invite you to go on this journey with me.

Download both bonuses for free:

5MinuteDiscipleship.com/bonus

Why a discipleship journal?

In Matthew 4:18-20, Jesus approached some fishermen on the shore of the Sea of Galilee and said, "Come, follow me." The Bible says, "At once they left their nets and followed him." This is the first time we see Jesus calling people to be his disciples.

The four Gospels tell the story of Jesus' earthly ministry, and the 12 disciples had a front-row seat. They witnessed the teaching, the miracles, and all the interactions with people. As followers of Jesus, they traveled with him, ate with him, and had access to personal conversations that others did not have. Somehow, along the way, they recorded what they saw and learned. As a result, we have the Books of Matthew, Mark, Luke, and John.

In the New Testament, the Greek word for disciple (*mathētēs*) means "student or apprentice." A disciple would follow a rabbi to learn, put their teaching into practice, and become like the rabbi.

If you are a Christian, you are a follower of Jesus, a disciple. We call this process of growing and becoming like Jesus: discipleship.

This discipleship journal can serve as a record of what you are learning and how you are growing spiritually. Imagine being able to look back at your spiritual progress and read what God has said to you and how you applied it in your daily life.

Before creating this journal, I read through dozens of journals that are designed for your personal devotions. Many seemed to be lacking two essential factors for spiritual growth: **a clear call to action and accountability**. Discipleship cannot happen without these two elements. Luke 11:28 says, *"But even more blessed are all who hear the word of God and put it into practice."* The personal application and talk it over sections of your daily practice might be the most crucial part of the journal.

Imagine someday, long after you have passed from this life, your grandchildren and great-grandchildren reading from your journals and learning how you grew close to Jesus and lived the life of a disciple.

Are you ready to do this? Let's get started.

How to Use this Journal

The journal is designed to help you grow every day in your relationship with God. Each day you will have the opportunity to reflect on God's Word, discern how you will apply the scripture, and determine your plan for sharing it with someone. At the end of the week, you will complete the weekly review and identify the progress you are making in your spiritual life.

What often hinders us is our lack of consistency. We start with great intentions, miss a few days, get discouraged, and give up. Let's decide upfront not to give in to this discouragement. We practice spiritual disciplines because we want to know God more. We are not checking boxes to fulfill our Christian duty.

This journal is a guide to help move you towards a deeper relationship with Christ. Life interrupts all of us. If you miss a day, just pick up where you left off and keep going. Consider keeping the journal in a visible place so you'll be reminded to spend time with God.

There are eight components of the daily journal. It should only take you a few minutes to complete the exercise, but as you do so, you are building good spiritual habits in your daily routine.

Scripture

From your daily Bible reading, write a verse or two that stands out to you. Look for verses that encourage, inspire, challenge, correct, and instruct. The practice of writing the scripture by hand reinforces retention and deeper understanding. Studies have shown that handwriting increases our potential for memorization.

What is God saying to me?

As you open the pages of the Bible, expect to hear God's voice. Develop the practice of listening for God to speak as you interact with the Scripture. Pause and ask God to talk to you. Write what you sense He is saying to you personally.

Application

The personal application of God's Word is how we grow to be more like Jesus. James 1:22 says, *"But don't just listen to God's word. You must do what it says. Otherwise, you are only fooling yourselves."* You will have the opportunity write how you will apply truth to your life. There are also boxes to check to indicate what action you will take.

- ☐ Step of faith
- ☐ Promise to believe
- ☐ Sin to confess
- ☐ Command to obey
- ☐ Prayer to pray
- ☐ Fear to surrender

Talk it over

This step could be easily ignored, but it has the potential to be the most crucial part of your spiritual disciplines. We grow best in the context of community, not isolation. Yet, most people do their personal devotions without any conversation or reflection with others. The "talk it over" step provides accountability, so we stay on track, and it helps us give and receive from others. Do not skip this valuable step!

Today, I am grateful for:

The Bible teaches us to "be thankful in all circumstances." Daily gratitude gives us much-needed perspective and focuses on what we have instead of what we do not have. Each day, develop the practice of identifying three things for which you want to give thanks.

Prayer

You have spent time in God's Word, listened for His voice, and identified how you would apply truth to your daily life. Now it is time to commit it all to God in prayer. Prayer is the expression of our heart. Write a prayer of gratitude, praise, petition, or commitment to God.

Memory Verse

Several Bible verses promise God's blessing for those who memorize and meditate on God's Word. Imagine having a verse each week that you remembered. Over a year, you would have learned 52 verses from God's Word. Select a verse, write it down, and practice reciting it.

Personal thoughts

Use this space to journal other thoughts you may have about your time in God's Word and how you will apply it to your life.

Weekly Review

Take a few minutes to review what God has done in your life over the past seven days. This step enables you to keep track of how you are growing spiritually. Sunday evening is an excellent time for this exercise. Review your progress. Did you miss some days in your journal this week? Decide how to get back on track.

As you review the past week, answer the following six questions.

How did you apply this week's scripture reading?

Where did you apply God's Word in your life in a practical way? Is God's Word shaping your character, your attitude, your actions, and your words? What did you do (or not do) this week, as a result of your time in the Bible.

What steps of faith did you take?

As we follow Jesus, the Holy Spirit is always asking us to trust Him by taking steps of faith. Where did you follow His leading, push past your current level of faith, and step out in obedience? Where are you being stretched to move forward with Christ?

Who did you share Christ with?

As Christians, we are called by God to share our faith and point people to Christ. True disciples of Jesus are actively involved in making other disciples. Did you invite someone to church, pray with someone, or tell them what Jesus has done in your life?

What prayers did God answer?

It is easy to overlook the prayers God answers for us daily. Think back over the past week and make a list of prayers God answered. Take time to thank God for what He is doing in your life.

Where do you see growth in your spiritual life?

The goal of the Christian life is spiritual maturity. In our character development, we are to become like Jesus. Where are you growing? Is your faith increasing? Is your love for God and others developing? Are you less anxious and afraid? Is your knowledge of God's Word expanding? Write down the ways you have grown spiritually this week.

Next week, with the help of the Holy Spirit:

Before you begin a new week, pray about where you need and want to grow. How can you be intentional this week to pursue a closer relationship with Jesus? Are there things you want to do? Perhaps there are things you want to stop doing. Either way, make an action plan for the week ahead.

My Prayer List

DATE: / /20   S   M   T   W   T   F   S

SCRIPTURE (Today's verse)

WHAT IS GOD SAYING TO ME? (Make it personal)

APPLICATION (What will I do?)

- ☐ Step of faith
- ☐ Promise to believe
- ☐ Sin to confess
- ☐ Command to obey
- ☐ Prayer to pray
- ☐ Fear to surrender

TALK IT OVER (Discuss this verse with a friend)

- • Who?   _____
- • When?   _____
- • Where?   _____
- • How?   _____

"If I am to wholly follow the Lord Jesus Christ, I must forsake everything that is contrary to Him". — A.W. Tozer

TODAY I AM GRATEFUL FOR:

1.

2.

3.

PRAYER

MEMORY VERSE:

PERSONAL THOUGHTS

_____

_____

_____

_____

_____

DATE: / /20 S M T W T F S

SCRIPTURE (Today's verse)

WHAT IS GOD SAYING TO ME? (Make it personal)

APPLICATION (What will I do?)
- ☐ Step of faith
- ☐ Promise to believe
- ☐ Sin to confess
- ☐ Command to obey
- ☐ Prayer to pray
- ☐ Fear to surrender

TALK IT OVER (Discuss this verse with a friend)

- Who?   _____
- When?   _____
- Where? _____
- How?   _____

"Discipleship is the process of becoming who Jesus would be if he were you."
— *Dallas Willard*

TODAY I AM GRATEFUL FOR:

1.

2.

3.

PRAYER

MEMORY VERSE:

PERSONAL THOUGHTS

_____

_____

_____

_____

_____

DATE: / /20   S M T W T F S

SCRIPTURE (Today's verse)

WHAT IS GOD SAYING TO ME? (Make it personal)

APPLICATION (What will I do?)

- ☐ Step of faith
- ☐ Promise to believe
- ☐ Sin to confess
- ☐ Command to obey
- ☐ Prayer to pray
- ☐ Fear to surrender

TALK IT OVER (Discuss this verse with a friend)

- Who?   _____
- When?   _____
- Where?   _____
- How?   _____

16

"Discipleship is not an option. Jesus says that if anyone would come after me, he must follow me." — Tim Keller

TODAY I AM GRATEFUL FOR:

1.

2.

3.

PRAYER

MEMORY VERSE:

PERSONAL THOUGHTS

_____

_____

_____

_____

_____

DATE: / /20 S M T W T F S

SCRIPTURE (Today's verse)

WHAT IS GOD SAYING TO ME? (Make it personal)

APPLICATION (What will I do?)
- ☐ Step of faith
- ☐ Promise to believe
- ☐ Sin to confess
- ☐ Command to obey
- ☐ Prayer to pray
- ☐ Fear to surrender

TALK IT OVER (Discuss this verse with a friend)

- Who?   _____
- When?   _____
- Where?   _____
- How?   _____

18

"Come, follow me, and I will show you how to fish for people. And they left their nets at once and followed him." — Matthew 4:19-20

TODAY I AM GRATEFUL FOR:

1.

2.

3.

PRAYER

MEMORY VERSE:

PERSONAL THOUGHTS

_____

_____

_____

_____

_____

DATE: / /20 S M T W T F S

SCRIPTURE (Today's verse)

WHAT IS GOD SAYING TO ME? (Make it personal)

APPLICATION (What will I do?)
- ☐ Step of faith
- ☐ Promise to believe
- ☐ Sin to confess
- ☐ Command to obey
- ☐ Prayer to pray
- ☐ Fear to surrender

TALK IT OVER (Discuss this verse with a friend)

- Who?   _____
- When?   _____
- Where?   _____
- How?   _____

TODAY I AM GRATEFUL FOR:

1.

2.

3.

PRAYER

MEMORY VERSE:

PERSONAL THOUGHTS

_____

_____

_____

_____

_____

DATE: / /20   S M T W T F S

SCRIPTURE (Today's verse)

WHAT IS GOD SAYING TO ME? (Make it personal)

APPLICATION (What will I do?)

☐ Step of faith
☐ Promise to believe
☐ Sin to confess
☐ Command to obey
☐ Prayer to pray
☐ Fear to surrender

TALK IT OVER (Discuss this verse with a friend)

- Who?   _____
- When?   _____
- Where?   _____
- How?   _____

22

"If you follow me, you won't have to walk in darkness, because you will have the light that leads to life." — John 8:12

TODAY I AM GRATEFUL FOR:

1.

2.

3.

PRAYER

MEMORY VERSE:

PERSONAL THOUGHTS

_____

_____

_____

_____

_____

DATE: / /20 S M T W T F S

SCRIPTURE (Today's verse)

WHAT IS GOD SAYING TO ME? (Make it personal)

APPLICATION (What will I do?)

- ☐ Step of faith
- ☐ Promise to believe
- ☐ Sin to confess
- ☐ Command to obey
- ☐ Prayer to pray
- ☐ Fear to surrender

TALK IT OVER (Discuss this verse with a friend)

- Who?   _____
- When?   _____
- Where?   _____
- How?   _____

24

"The Christian life is the discipled life and the discipling life."
— Mark Dever

TODAY I AM GRATEFUL FOR:

1.

2.

3.

PRAYER

MEMORY VERSE:

PERSONAL THOUGHTS

_____

_____

_____

_____

_____

Weekly Review

How did you apply this week's scripture reading?

What steps of faith did you take?

Who did you share Christ with?

What prayers did God answer?

Where do you see growth in your spiritual life?

Next week, with the help of the Holy Spirit:

☐ I will:

☐ I will not:

DATE: /   /20   S   M   T   W   T   F   S

SCRIPTURE (Today's verse)

WHAT IS GOD SAYING TO ME? (Make it personal)

APPLICATION (What will I do?)

- ☐   Step of faith
- ☐   Promise to believe
- ☐   Sin to confess
- ☐   Command to obey
- ☐   Prayer to pray
- ☐   Fear to surrender

TALK IT OVER (Discuss this verse with a friend)

- • Who?   _____
- • When?   _____
- • Where?   _____
- • How?   _____

28

"Oh, how I love your instructions! I think about them all day long." - Psalm 119:97

TODAY I AM GRATEFUL FOR:

1.

2.

3.

PRAYER

MEMORY VERSE:

PERSONAL THOUGHTS

_____

_____

_____

_____

_____

DATE: / /20 S M T W T F S

SCRIPTURE (Today's verse)

WHAT IS GOD SAYING TO ME? (Make it personal)

APPLICATION (What will I do?)
☐ Step of faith
☐ Promise to believe
☐ Sin to confess
☐ Command to obey
☐ Prayer to pray
☐ Fear to surrender

TALK IT OVER (Discuss this verse with a friend)

- Who? _____
- When? _____
- Where? _____
- How? _____

"Anyone who wants to serve me must follow me, because my servants must be where I am. And the Father will honor anyone who serves me." — John 12:26

TODAY I AM GRATEFUL FOR:

1.

2.

3.

PRAYER

MEMORY VERSE:

PERSONAL THOUGHTS

_____
_____
_____
_____
_____

DATE: / /20 S M T W T F S

SCRIPTURE (Today's verse)

WHAT IS GOD SAYING TO ME? (Make it personal)

APPLICATION (What will I do?)
- ☐ Step of faith
- ☐ Promise to believe
- ☐ Sin to confess
- ☐ Command to obey
- ☐ Prayer to pray
- ☐ Fear to surrender

TALK IT OVER (Discuss this verse with a friend)

- Who? _____
- When? _____
- Where? _____
- How? _____

"The one indispensable requirement for producing godly, mature Christians is godly, mature Christians." – Kevin DeYoung

TODAY I AM GRATEFUL FOR:

1.

2.

3.

PRAYER

MEMORY VERSE:

PERSONAL THOUGHTS

_____

_____

_____

_____

_____

DATE: / /20   S M T W T F S

SCRIPTURE (Today's verse)

WHAT IS GOD SAYING TO ME? (Make it personal)

APPLICATION (What will I do?)
- ☐ Step of faith
- ☐ Promise to believe
- ☐ Sin to confess
- ☐ Command to obey
- ☐ Prayer to pray
- ☐ Fear to surrender

TALK IT OVER (Discuss this verse with a friend)

- Who?   _____
- When?   _____
- Where?   _____
- How?   _____

"Therefore, go and make disciples of all the nations, baptizing them in the name of the Father and the Son and the Holy Spirit." – Matthew 28:19

TODAY I AM GRATEFUL FOR:

1.

2.

3.

PRAYER

MEMORY VERSE:

PERSONAL THOUGHTS

_____

_____

_____

_____

_____

DATE: /   /20   S   M   T   W   T   F   S

SCRIPTURE (Today's verse)

WHAT IS GOD SAYING TO ME? (Make it personal)

APPLICATION (What will I do?)

☐   Step of faith
☐   Promise to believe
☐   Sin to confess
☐   Command to obey
☐   Prayer to pray
☐   Fear to surrender

TALK IT OVER (Discuss this verse with a friend)

- Who?   _____
- When?   _____
- Where?   _____
- How?   _____

"Our first discipleship priority is with those sitting around our dining room table."
— Loren Hicks

TODAY I AM GRATEFUL FOR:

1.

2.

3.

PRAYER

MEMORY VERSE:

PERSONAL THOUGHTS

_____

_____

_____

_____

_____

DATE: /   /20   S   M   T   W   T   F   S

SCRIPTURE (Today's verse)

WHAT IS GOD SAYING TO ME? (Make it personal)

APPLICATION (What will I do?)
- ☐ Step of faith
- ☐ Promise to believe
- ☐ Sin to confess
- ☐ Command to obey
- ☐ Prayer to pray
- ☐ Fear to surrender

TALK IT OVER (Discuss this verse with a friend)

- Who?   _____
- When?   _____
- Where?   _____
- How?   _____

"When you produce much fruit, you are my true disciples. This brings great glory to my Father." – John 15:8

TODAY I AM GRATEFUL FOR:

1.

2.

3.

PRAYER

MEMORY VERSE:

PERSONAL THOUGHTS

_____

_____

_____

_____

_____

DATE: / /20 S M T W T F S

SCRIPTURE (Today's verse)

WHAT IS GOD SAYING TO ME? (Make it personal)

APPLICATION (What will I do?)
- ☐ Step of faith
- ☐ Promise to believe
- ☐ Sin to confess
- ☐ Command to obey
- ☐ Prayer to pray
- ☐ Fear to surrender

TALK IT OVER (Discuss this verse with a friend)

- Who? _____
- When? _____
- Where? _____
- How? _____

"To be a disciple is to be committed to Jesus Christ as Savior and Lord and committed to following Him every day." – Billy Graham

TODAY I AM GRATEFUL FOR:

1.

2.

3.

PRAYER

MEMORY VERSE:

PERSONAL THOUGHTS

_____
_____
_____
_____
_____

Weekly Review

How did you apply this week's scripture reading?

What steps of faith did you take?

Who did you share Christ with?

What prayers did God answer?

Where do you see growth in your spiritual life?

Next week, with the help of the Holy Spirit:

☐ I will:

☐ I will not:

DATE: / /20 S M T W T F S

SCRIPTURE (Today's verse)

WHAT IS GOD SAYING TO ME? (Make it personal)

APPLICATION (What will I do?)
☐ Step of faith
☐ Promise to believe
☐ Sin to confess
☐ Command to obey
☐ Prayer to pray
☐ Fear to surrender

TALK IT OVER (Discuss this verse with a friend)

- Who? _____
- When? _____
- Where? _____
- How? _____

"If any of you wants to be my follower, you must give up your own way, take up your cross, and follow me." - Mark 8:34

TODAY I AM GRATEFUL FOR:

1.

2.

3.

PRAYER

MEMORY VERSE:

PERSONAL THOUGHTS

_____

_____

_____

_____

_____

DATE: / /20 S M T W T F S

SCRIPTURE (Today's verse)

WHAT IS GOD SAYING TO ME? (Make it personal)

APPLICATION (What will I do?)

☐ Step of faith
☐ Promise to believe
☐ Sin to confess
☐ Command to obey
☐ Prayer to pray
☐ Fear to surrender

TALK IT OVER (Discuss this verse with a friend)

- Who? _____
- When? _____
- Where? _____
- How? _____

46

"Making disciples of Jesus is the overflow of the delight in being disciples of Jesus."
- David Platt

TODAY I AM GRATEFUL FOR:

1.

2.

3.

PRAYER

MEMORY VERSE:

PERSONAL THOUGHTS

_____

_____

_____

_____

_____

DATE: /   /20   S   M   T   W   T   F   S

SCRIPTURE (Today's verse)

WHAT IS GOD SAYING TO ME? (Make it personal)

APPLICATION (What will I do?)
- ☐ Step of faith
- ☐ Promise to believe
- ☐ Sin to confess
- ☐ Command to obey
- ☐ Prayer to pray
- ☐ Fear to surrender

TALK IT OVER (Discuss this verse with a friend)

- Who?   _____
- When?   _____
- Where?   _____
- How?   _____

48

"Be a good worker, one who does not need to be ashamed and who correctly explains the word of truth." - 2 Timothy 2:15

TODAY I AM GRATEFUL FOR:

1.

2.

3.

PRAYER

MEMORY VERSE:

PERSONAL THOUGHTS

_____

_____

_____

_____

_____

DATE: / /20   S M T W T F S

SCRIPTURE (Today's verse)

WHAT IS GOD SAYING TO ME? (Make it personal)

APPLICATION (What will I do?)
- ☐ Step of faith
- ☐ Promise to believe
- ☐ Sin to confess
- ☐ Command to obey
- ☐ Prayer to pray
- ☐ Fear to surrender

TALK IT OVER (Discuss this verse with a friend)

- Who?   _____
- When?   _____
- Where?   _____
- How?   _____

"Christian discipleship is a decision to walk in his ways, steadily and firmly. It is the way of life we were created for." - Eugene H. Peterson

TODAY I AM GRATEFUL FOR:

1.

2.

3.

PRAYER

MEMORY VERSE:

PERSONAL THOUGHTS

_____

_____

_____

_____

_____

DATE: / /20   S M T W T F S

SCRIPTURE (Today's verse)

WHAT IS GOD SAYING TO ME? (Make it personal)

APPLICATION (What will I do?)

- ☐ Step of faith
- ☐ Promise to believe
- ☐ Sin to confess
- ☐ Command to obey
- ☐ Prayer to pray
- ☐ Fear to surrender

TALK IT OVER (Discuss this verse with a friend)

- Who?   _____
- When?   _____
- Where?   _____
- How?   _____

"Don't you realize that your body is the temple of the Holy Spirit, who lives in you and was given to you by God? You do not belong to yourself" - 1 Corinthians 6:19

TODAY I AM GRATEFUL FOR:

1.

2.

3.

PRAYER

MEMORY VERSE:

PERSONAL THOUGHTS

_____

_____

_____

_____

_____

DATE: /   /20   S   M   T   W   T   F   S

SCRIPTURE (Today's verse)

WHAT IS GOD SAYING TO ME? (Make it personal)

APPLICATION (What will I do?)

- ☐ Step of faith
- ☐ Promise to believe
- ☐ Sin to confess
- ☐ Command to obey
- ☐ Prayer to pray
- ☐ Fear to surrender

TALK IT OVER (Discuss this verse with a friend)

- Who?   _____
- When?   _____
- Where?   _____
- How?   _____

"Christianity without discipleship is always Christianity without Christ."
- Dietrich Bonhoeffer

TODAY I AM GRATEFUL FOR:

1.

2.

3.

PRAYER

MEMORY VERSE:

PERSONAL THOUGHTS

_____

_____

_____

_____

_____

DATE: / /20 S M T W T F S

SCRIPTURE (Today's verse)

WHAT IS GOD SAYING TO ME? (Make it personal)

APPLICATION (What will I do?)
- ☐ Step of faith
- ☐ Promise to believe
- ☐ Sin to confess
- ☐ Command to obey
- ☐ Prayer to pray
- ☐ Fear to surrender

TALK IT OVER (Discuss this verse with a friend)

- Who? _____
- When? _____
- Where? _____
- How? _____

"But you will receive power when the Holy Spirit comes upon you. And you will be my witnesses, telling people about me everywhere" - Acts 1:8

TODAY I AM GRATEFUL FOR:

1.

2.

3.

PRAYER

MEMORY VERSE:

PERSONAL THOUGHTS

_____

_____

_____

_____

_____

Weekly Review

How did you apply this week's scripture reading?

What steps of faith did you take?

Who did you share Christ with?

What prayers did God answer?

Where do you see growth in your spiritual life?

Next week, with the help of the Holy Spirit:

☐ I will:

☐ I will not:

DATE: / /20 S M T W T F S

SCRIPTURE (Today's verse)

WHAT IS GOD SAYING TO ME? (Make it personal)

APPLICATION (What will I do?)

☐ Step of faith
☐ Promise to believe
☐ Sin to confess
☐ Command to obey
☐ Prayer to pray
☐ Fear to surrender

TALK IT OVER (Discuss this verse with a friend)

- Who? _____
- When? _____
- Where? _____
- How? _____

60

"Discipleship isn't a program or an event; it's a way of life. It's not for a limited time, but for our whole life." - Bill Hull

TODAY I AM GRATEFUL FOR:

1.

2.

3.

PRAYER

MEMORY VERSE:

PERSONAL THOUGHTS

_____

_____

_____

_____

_____

DATE: / /20   S M T W T F S

SCRIPTURE (Today's verse)

WHAT IS GOD SAYING TO ME? (Make it personal)

APPLICATION (What will I do?)
- ☐ Step of faith
- ☐ Promise to believe
- ☐ Sin to confess
- ☐ Command to obey
- ☐ Prayer to pray
- ☐ Fear to surrender

TALK IT OVER (Discuss this verse with a friend)

- Who?   _____
- When?   _____
- Where?   _____
- How?   _____

"No one can serve two masters. For you will hate one and love the other; you will be devoted to one and despise the other." - Matthew 6:24

TODAY I AM GRATEFUL FOR:

1.

2.

3.

PRAYER

MEMORY VERSE:

PERSONAL THOUGHTS

_____
_____
_____
_____
_____

DATE: / /20   S M T W T F S

SCRIPTURE (Today's verse)

WHAT IS GOD SAYING TO ME? (Make it personal)

APPLICATION (What will I do?)

- ☐ Step of faith
- ☐ Promise to believe
- ☐ Sin to confess
- ☐ Command to obey
- ☐ Prayer to pray
- ☐ Fear to surrender

TALK IT OVER (Discuss this verse with a friend)

- • Who?   _____
- • When?   _____
- • Where?   _____
- • How?   _____

"Only a disciple can make a disciple." - A.W. Tozer

TODAY I AM GRATEFUL FOR:

1.

2.

3.

PRAYER

MEMORY VERSE:

PERSONAL THOUGHTS

_____

_____

_____

_____

_____

DATE: / /20   S M T W T F S

SCRIPTURE (Today's verse)

WHAT IS GOD SAYING TO ME? (Make it personal)

APPLICATION (What will I do?)

☐ Step of faith
☐ Promise to believe
☐ Sin to confess
☐ Command to obey
☐ Prayer to pray
☐ Fear to surrender

TALK IT OVER (Discuss this verse with a friend)

- Who?   _____
- When?   _____
- Where?   _____
- How?   _____

"Your love for one another will prove to the world that you are my disciples."
- John 13:35

TODAY I AM GRATEFUL FOR:

1.

2.

3.

PRAYER

MEMORY VERSE:

PERSONAL THOUGHTS

_____

_____

_____

_____

_____

DATE: / /20 S M T W T F S

SCRIPTURE (Today's verse)

WHAT IS GOD SAYING TO ME? (Make it personal)

APPLICATION (What will I do?)
- ☐ Step of faith
- ☐ Promise to believe
- ☐ Sin to confess
- ☐ Command to obey
- ☐ Prayer to pray
- ☐ Fear to surrender

TALK IT OVER (Discuss this verse with a friend)

- Who?   _____
- When?   _____
- Where?   _____
- How?   _____

"Until you have given up yourself to Him you will not have a real self." - C.S. Lewis

TODAY I AM GRATEFUL FOR:

1.

2.

3.

PRAYER

MEMORY VERSE:

PERSONAL THOUGHTS

_____

_____

_____

_____

_____

DATE: / /20   S M T W T F S

SCRIPTURE (Today's verse)

WHAT IS GOD SAYING TO ME? (Make it personal)

APPLICATION (What will I do?)
- ☐ Step of faith
- ☐ Promise to believe
- ☐ Sin to confess
- ☐ Command to obey
- ☐ Prayer to pray
- ☐ Fear to surrender

TALK IT OVER (Discuss this verse with a friend)

- Who?   _____
- When?   _____
- Where?   _____
- How?   _____

"But don't just listen to God's word. You must do what it says. Otherwise, you are only fooling yourselves." - James 1:22

TODAY I AM GRATEFUL FOR:

1.

2.

3.

PRAYER

MEMORY VERSE:

PERSONAL THOUGHTS

_____
_____
_____
_____
_____

DATE: / /20   S M T W T F S

SCRIPTURE (Today's verse)

WHAT IS GOD SAYING TO ME? (Make it personal)

APPLICATION (What will I do?)
- ☐ Step of faith
- ☐ Promise to believe
- ☐ Sin to confess
- ☐ Command to obey
- ☐ Prayer to pray
- ☐ Fear to surrender

TALK IT OVER (Discuss this verse with a friend)

- Who?   _____
- When?   _____
- Where?   _____
- How?   _____

"Discipleship entails a whole-hearted devotion to the Lord alone, a willingness to obey His commands in everything." - John McArthur

TODAY I AM GRATEFUL FOR:

1.

2.

3.

PRAYER

MEMORY VERSE:

PERSONAL THOUGHTS

_____

_____

_____

_____

_____

Weekly Review

How did you apply this week's scripture reading?

What steps of faith did you take?

Who did you share Christ with?

What prayers did God answer?

Where do you see growth in your spiritual life?

Next week, with the help of the Holy Spirit:

☐ I will:

☐ I will not:

DATE: / /20   S   M   T   W   T   F   S

SCRIPTURE (Today's verse)

WHAT IS GOD SAYING TO ME? (Make it personal)

APPLICATION (What will I do?)
- ☐ Step of faith
- ☐ Promise to believe
- ☐ Sin to confess
- ☐ Command to obey
- ☐ Prayer to pray
- ☐ Fear to surrender

TALK IT OVER (Discuss this verse with a friend)

- Who?   _____
- When?   _____
- Where?   _____
- How?   _____

"Whoever wants to be first must take last place and be the servant of everyone else."
- Mark 9:35

TODAY I AM GRATEFUL FOR:

1.

2.

3.

PRAYER

MEMORY VERSE:

PERSONAL THOUGHTS

_____

_____

_____

_____

_____

DATE: / /20   S M T W T F S

SCRIPTURE (Today's verse)

WHAT IS GOD SAYING TO ME? (Make it personal)

APPLICATION (What will I do?)

- ☐ Step of faith
- ☐ Promise to believe
- ☐ Sin to confess
- ☐ Command to obey
- ☐ Prayer to pray
- ☐ Fear to surrender

TALK IT OVER (Discuss this verse with a friend)

- Who?   _____
- When?   _____
- Where?   _____
- How?   _____

"You will know as much of God, and only as much of God, as you are willing to put into practice." - Eric Liddell

TODAY I AM GRATEFUL FOR:

1.

2.

3.

PRAYER

MEMORY VERSE:

PERSONAL THOUGHTS

_____
_____
_____
_____
_____

DATE: / /20 S M T W T F S

SCRIPTURE (Today's verse)

WHAT IS GOD SAYING TO ME? (Make it personal)

APPLICATION (What will I do?)

☐ Step of faith
☐ Promise to believe
☐ Sin to confess
☐ Command to obey
☐ Prayer to pray
☐ Fear to surrender

TALK IT OVER (Discuss this verse with a friend)

- Who? _____
- When? _____
- Where? _____
- How? _____

"Jesus replied, "All who love me will do what I say. My Father will love them, and we will come and make our home with each of them." - John 14:23

TODAY I AM GRATEFUL FOR:

1.

2.

3.

PRAYER

MEMORY VERSE:

PERSONAL THOUGHTS

_____

_____

_____

_____

_____

DATE: /   /20   S   M   T   W   T   F   S

SCRIPTURE (Today's verse)

WHAT IS GOD SAYING TO ME? (Make it personal)

APPLICATION (What will I do?)
- ☐ Step of faith
- ☐ Promise to believe
- ☐ Sin to confess
- ☐ Command to obey
- ☐ Prayer to pray
- ☐ Fear to surrender

TALK IT OVER (Discuss this verse with a friend)

- Who?   _____
- When?   _____
- Where?   _____
- How?   _____

"One does not surrender a life in an instant. That which is lifelong can only be surrendered in a lifetime." - Elisabeth Elliott

TODAY I AM GRATEFUL FOR:

1.

2.

3.

PRAYER

MEMORY VERSE:

PERSONAL THOUGHTS

_____

_____

_____

_____

_____

DATE: / /20 S M T W T F S

SCRIPTURE (Today's verse)

WHAT IS GOD SAYING TO ME? (Make it personal)

APPLICATION (What will I do?)
- ☐ Step of faith
- ☐ Promise to believe
- ☐ Sin to confess
- ☐ Command to obey
- ☐ Prayer to pray
- ☐ Fear to surrender

TALK IT OVER (Discuss this verse with a friend)

- Who? _____
- When? _____
- Where? _____
- How? _____

84

"And what do you benefit if you gain the whole world but lose your own soul? Is anything worth more than your soul?" - Matthew 16:26

TODAY I AM GRATEFUL FOR:

1.

2.

3.

PRAYER

MEMORY VERSE:

PERSONAL THOUGHTS

_____

_____

_____

_____

_____

DATE: / /20   S   M   T   W   T   F   S

SCRIPTURE (Today's verse)

WHAT IS GOD SAYING TO ME? (Make it personal)

APPLICATION (What will I do?)
- ☐ Step of faith
- ☐ Promise to believe
- ☐ Sin to confess
- ☐ Command to obey
- ☐ Prayer to pray
- ☐ Fear to surrender

TALK IT OVER (Discuss this verse with a friend)

- Who?   _____
- When?   _____
- Where?   _____
- How?   _____

"The one indispensable requirement for producing godly, mature Christians is godly, mature Christians." - Kevin DeYoung

TODAY I AM GRATEFUL FOR:

1.

2.

3.

PRAYER

MEMORY VERSE:

PERSONAL THOUGHTS

_____

_____

_____

_____

_____

DATE: / /20 S M T W T F S

SCRIPTURE (Today's verse)

WHAT IS GOD SAYING TO ME? (Make it personal)

APPLICATION (What will I do?)
- ☐ Step of faith
- ☐ Promise to believe
- ☐ Sin to confess
- ☐ Command to obey
- ☐ Prayer to pray
- ☐ Fear to surrender

TALK IT OVER (Discuss this verse with a friend)

- Who? _____
- When? _____
- Where? _____
- How? _____

"Discipleship demands that we be lifelong learners and that we commit to constant growth in spiritual maturity." - Michael Spencer

TODAY I AM GRATEFUL FOR:

1.

2.

3.

PRAYER

MEMORY VERSE:

PERSONAL THOUGHTS

_____

_____

_____

_____

_____

Weekly Review

How did you apply this week's scripture reading?

What steps of faith did you take?

Who did you share Christ with?

What prayers did God answer?

Where do you see growth in your spiritual life?

Next week, with the help of the Holy Spirit:

☐   I will:

☐   I will not:

DATE: / /20 S M T W T F S

SCRIPTURE (Today's verse)

WHAT IS GOD SAYING TO ME? (Make it personal)

APPLICATION (What will I do?)

- ☐ Step of faith
- ☐ Promise to believe
- ☐ Sin to confess
- ☐ Command to obey
- ☐ Prayer to pray
- ☐ Fear to surrender

TALK IT OVER (Discuss this verse with a friend)

- Who?   _____
- When?   _____
- Where?   _____
- How?   _____

"So humble yourselves before God. Resist the devil, and he will flee from you."
- James 4:7

TODAY I AM GRATEFUL FOR:

1.

2.

3.

PRAYER

MEMORY VERSE:

PERSONAL THOUGHTS

_____

_____

_____

_____

_____

DATE: / /20   S M T W T F S

SCRIPTURE (Today's verse)

WHAT IS GOD SAYING TO ME? (Make it personal)

APPLICATION (What will I do?)
- ☐ Step of faith
- ☐ Promise to believe
- ☐ Sin to confess
- ☐ Command to obey
- ☐ Prayer to pray
- ☐ Fear to surrender

TALK IT OVER (Discuss this verse with a friend)

- Who?   _____
- When?   _____
- Where?   _____
- How?   _____

94

"Jesus always comes asking disciples to follow him--not merely 'accept him,' not merely 'believe in him,' not merely 'worship him,' but to follow him." - Lee Camp

TODAY I AM GRATEFUL FOR:

1.

2.

3.

PRAYER

MEMORY VERSE:

PERSONAL THOUGHTS

_____

_____

_____

_____

_____

DATE: / /20 S M T W T F S

SCRIPTURE (Today's verse)

WHAT IS GOD SAYING TO ME? (Make it personal)

APPLICATION (What will I do?)

- ☐ Step of faith
- ☐ Promise to believe
- ☐ Sin to confess
- ☐ Command to obey
- ☐ Prayer to pray
- ☐ Fear to surrender

TALK IT OVER (Discuss this verse with a friend)

- Who? _____
- When? _____
- Where? _____
- How? _____

"You can enter God's Kingdom only through the narrow gate. The highway to hell is broad, and its gate is wide for the many who choose that way." - Matthew 7:13

TODAY I AM GRATEFUL FOR:

1.

2.

3.

PRAYER

MEMORY VERSE:

PERSONAL THOUGHTS

_____
_____
_____
_____
_____

DATE: /   /20   S M T W T F S

SCRIPTURE (Today's verse)

WHAT IS GOD SAYING TO ME? (Make it personal)

APPLICATION (What will I do?)
- ☐ Step of faith
- ☐ Promise to believe
- ☐ Sin to confess
- ☐ Command to obey
- ☐ Prayer to pray
- ☐ Fear to surrender

TALK IT OVER (Discuss this verse with a friend)

- Who?   _____
- When?   _____
- Where?   _____
- How?   _____

"Transformation is a process, a journey, not a one-time decision." - David Kinnaman

TODAY I AM GRATEFUL FOR:

1.

2.

3.

PRAYER

MEMORY VERSE:

PERSONAL THOUGHTS

_____
_____
_____
_____
_____

DATE: / /20   S   M   T   W   T   F   S

SCRIPTURE (Today's verse)

WHAT IS GOD SAYING TO ME? (Make it personal)

APPLICATION (What will I do?)
- ☐ Step of faith
- ☐ Promise to believe
- ☐ Sin to confess
- ☐ Command to obey
- ☐ Prayer to pray
- ☐ Fear to surrender

TALK IT OVER (Discuss this verse with a friend)

- Who?   _____
- When?   _____
- Where?   _____
- How?   _____

"Not everyone who calls out to me, 'Lord! Lord!' will enter the Kingdom of Heaven. Only those who actually do the will of my Father in heaven will enter." - Matthew 7:21

TODAY I AM GRATEFUL FOR:

1.

2.

3.

PRAYER

MEMORY VERSE:

PERSONAL THOUGHTS

_____

_____

_____

_____

_____

DATE: / /20   S M T W T F S

SCRIPTURE (Today's verse)

WHAT IS GOD SAYING TO ME? (Make it personal)

APPLICATION (What will I do?)

- ☐ Step of faith
- ☐ Promise to believe
- ☐ Sin to confess
- ☐ Command to obey
- ☐ Prayer to pray
- ☐ Fear to surrender

TALK IT OVER (Discuss this verse with a friend)

- Who?   _____
- When?   _____
- Where?   _____
- How?   _____

"Everything in Scripture is either preparation for the Gospel, presentation of the Gospel, or participation in the Gospel." - Dave Harvey

TODAY I AM GRATEFUL FOR:

1.

2.

3.

PRAYER

MEMORY VERSE:

PERSONAL THOUGHTS

_____

_____

_____

_____

_____

DATE: / /20 S M T W T F S

SCRIPTURE (Today's verse)

WHAT IS GOD SAYING TO ME? (Make it personal)

APPLICATION (What will I do?)
☐ Step of faith
☐ Promise to believe
☐ Sin to confess
☐ Command to obey
☐ Prayer to pray
☐ Fear to surrender

TALK IT OVER (Discuss this verse with a friend)

- Who? _____
- When? _____
- Where? _____
- How? _____

"For you have been called to live in freedom, my brothers and sisters. But don't use your freedom to satisfy your sinful nature." - Galatians 5:13

TODAY I AM GRATEFUL FOR:

1.

2.

3.

PRAYER

MEMORY VERSE:

PERSONAL THOUGHTS

_____

_____

_____

_____

_____

Weekly Review

How did you apply this week's scripture reading?

What steps of faith did you take?

Who did you share Christ with?

What prayers did God answer?

Where do you see growth in your spiritual life?

Next week, with the help of the Holy Spirit:

☐   I will:

☐   I will not:

DATE: / /20 S M T W T F S

SCRIPTURE (Today's verse)

WHAT IS GOD SAYING TO ME? (Make it personal)

APPLICATION (What will I do?)

☐ Step of faith
☐ Promise to believe
☐ Sin to confess
☐ Command to obey
☐ Prayer to pray
☐ Fear to surrender

TALK IT OVER (Discuss this verse with a friend)

- Who? _____
- When? _____
- Where? _____
- How? _____

108

"The Christian life does not just evolve. It also requires specific decisions and public commitments to deepen our faith and obedience." - Mark Galli

TODAY I AM GRATEFUL FOR:

1.

2.

3.

PRAYER

MEMORY VERSE:

PERSONAL THOUGHTS

_____

_____

_____

_____

_____

DATE: /   /20   S   M   T   W   T   F   S

SCRIPTURE (Today's verse)

WHAT IS GOD SAYING TO ME? (Make it personal)

APPLICATION (What will I do?)

- ☐ Step of faith
- ☐ Promise to believe
- ☐ Sin to confess
- ☐ Command to obey
- ☐ Prayer to pray
- ☐ Fear to surrender

TALK IT OVER (Discuss this verse with a friend)

- Who?   _____
- When?   _____
- Where?   _____
- How?   _____

"Jesus replied, "But even more blessed are all who hear the word of God and put it into practice."- Luke 11:28

TODAY I AM GRATEFUL FOR:

1.

2.

3.

PRAYER

MEMORY VERSE:

PERSONAL THOUGHTS

_____

_____

_____

_____

_____

DATE: /   /20   S   M   T   W   T   F   S

SCRIPTURE (Today's verse)

WHAT IS GOD SAYING TO ME? (Make it personal)

APPLICATION (What will I do?)

☐   Step of faith
☐   Promise to believe
☐   Sin to confess
☐   Command to obey
☐   Prayer to pray
☐   Fear to surrender

TALK IT OVER (Discuss this verse with a friend)

- Who?   _____
- When?   _____
- Where?   _____
- How?   _____

"For the Christian serves the fellowship of the Body of Christ, and he cannot hide it from the world. He is called out of the world to follow Christ." - Dietrich Bonhoeffer

TODAY I AM GRATEFUL FOR:

1.

2.

3.

PRAYER

MEMORY VERSE:

PERSONAL THOUGHTS

DATE: / /20 S M T W T F S

SCRIPTURE (Today's verse)

WHAT IS GOD SAYING TO ME? (Make it personal)

APPLICATION (What will I do?)

☐ Step of faith
☐ Promise to believe
☐ Sin to confess
☐ Command to obey
☐ Prayer to pray
☐ Fear to surrender

TALK IT OVER (Discuss this verse with a friend)

- Who?   _____
- When?   _____
- Where?   _____
- How?   _____

"For it is by believing in your heart that you are made right with God, and it is by openly declaring your faith that you are saved." - Romans 10:10

TODAY I AM GRATEFUL FOR:

1.

2.

3.

PRAYER

MEMORY VERSE:

PERSONAL THOUGHTS

_____
_____
_____
_____
_____

DATE: / /20 S M T W T F S

SCRIPTURE (Today's verse)

WHAT IS GOD SAYING TO ME? (Make it personal)

APPLICATION (What will I do?)
- ☐ Step of faith
- ☐ Promise to believe
- ☐ Sin to confess
- ☐ Command to obey
- ☐ Prayer to pray
- ☐ Fear to surrender

TALK IT OVER (Discuss this verse with a friend)

- Who?   _____
- When?   _____
- Where?   _____
- How?   _____

116

"So you must live as God's obedient children. Don't slip back into your old ways of living to satisfy your own desires. You didn't know any better then." - 1 Peter 1:14

TODAY I AM GRATEFUL FOR:

1.

2.

3.

PRAYER

MEMORY VERSE:

PERSONAL THOUGHTS

DATE: / /20 S M T W T F S

SCRIPTURE (Today's verse)

WHAT IS GOD SAYING TO ME? (Make it personal)

APPLICATION (What will I do?)
- ☐ Step of faith
- ☐ Promise to believe
- ☐ Sin to confess
- ☐ Command to obey
- ☐ Prayer to pray
- ☐ Fear to surrender

TALK IT OVER (Discuss this verse with a friend)

- Who?   _____
- When?   _____
- Where?   _____
- How?   _____

118

"We must say yes to the gospel, and that yes is manifested in life as lived daily; or we can say no even by our inactivity." - Jacqueline Grant

TODAY I AM GRATEFUL FOR:

1.

2.

3.

PRAYER

MEMORY VERSE:

PERSONAL THOUGHTS

_____

_____

_____

_____

_____

DATE: / /20 S M T W T F S

SCRIPTURE (Today's verse)

WHAT IS GOD SAYING TO ME? (Make it personal)

APPLICATION (What will I do?)
- ☐ Step of faith
- ☐ Promise to believe
- ☐ Sin to confess
- ☐ Command to obey
- ☐ Prayer to pray
- ☐ Fear to surrender

TALK IT OVER (Discuss this verse with a friend)

- Who? _____
- When? _____
- Where? _____
- How? _____

120

"We died and were buried with Christ by baptism. And just as Christ was raised from the dead by the glorious power of the Father, now we also may live new lives." Romans 6:4

TODAY I AM GRATEFUL FOR:

1.

2.

3.

PRAYER

MEMORY VERSE:

PERSONAL THOUGHTS

_____

_____

_____

_____

_____

Weekly Review

How did you apply this week's scripture reading?

What steps of faith did you take?

Who did you share Christ with?

What prayers did God answer?

Where do you see growth in your spiritual life?

Next week, with the help of the Holy Spirit:

☐ I will:

☐ I will not:

DATE: /   /20   S   M   T   W   T   F   S

SCRIPTURE (Today's verse)

WHAT IS GOD SAYING TO ME? (Make it personal)

APPLICATION (What will I do?)
- ☐   Step of faith
- ☐   Promise to believe
- ☐   Sin to confess
- ☐   Command to obey
- ☐   Prayer to pray
- ☐   Fear to surrender

TALK IT OVER (Discuss this verse with a friend)

- Who?   _____
- When?   _____
- Where?   _____
- How?   _____

124

"Discipleship is intentionally equipping believers with the Word of God through accountable relationships empowered by the Holy Spirit." - Kandi Gallaty

TODAY I AM GRATEFUL FOR:

1.

2.

3.

PRAYER

MEMORY VERSE:

PERSONAL THOUGHTS

_____
_____
_____
_____
_____

DATE: /   /20   S   M   T   W   T   F   S

SCRIPTURE (Today's verse)

WHAT IS GOD SAYING TO ME? (Make it personal)

APPLICATION (What will I do?)

- ☐ Step of faith
- ☐ Promise to believe
- ☐ Sin to confess
- ☐ Command to obey
- ☐ Prayer to pray
- ☐ Fear to surrender

TALK IT OVER (Discuss this verse with a friend)

- Who? _____
- When? _____
- Where? _____
- How? _____

"We destroy every proud obstacle that keeps people from knowing God. We capture their rebellious thoughts and teach them to obey Christ." - 2 Corinthians 10:5

TODAY I AM GRATEFUL FOR:

1.

2.

3.

PRAYER

MEMORY VERSE:

PERSONAL THOUGHTS

DATE: / /20 S M T W T F S

SCRIPTURE (Today's verse)

WHAT IS GOD SAYING TO ME? (Make it personal)

APPLICATION (What will I do?)

☐ Step of faith
☐ Promise to believe
☐ Sin to confess
☐ Command to obey
☐ Prayer to pray
☐ Fear to surrender

TALK IT OVER (Discuss this verse with a friend)

- Who? _____
- When? _____
- Where? _____
- How? _____

128

"Parenthood is a high calling. It's our first mission field and our first place for discipleship. I think that it is one of the toughest places to make disciples." - Mandi Hart

TODAY I AM GRATEFUL FOR:

1.

2.

3.

PRAYER

MEMORY VERSE:

PERSONAL THOUGHTS

_____
_____
_____
_____
_____

DATE: / /20   S M T W T F S

SCRIPTURE (Today's verse)

WHAT IS GOD SAYING TO ME? (Make it personal)

APPLICATION (What will I do?)

☐ Step of faith
☐ Promise to believe
☐ Sin to confess
☐ Command to obey
☐ Prayer to pray
☐ Fear to surrender

TALK IT OVER (Discuss this verse with a friend)

- Who?   _____
- When?   _____
- Where?   _____
- How?   _____

"Radical discipleship takes place in a relational environment where people learn what it means to be a follower of Jesus." - Jonathan Hayashi

TODAY I AM GRATEFUL FOR:

1.

2.

3.

PRAYER

MEMORY VERSE:

PERSONAL THOUGHTS

_____

_____

_____

_____

_____

DATE: / /20 S M T W T F S

SCRIPTURE (Today's verse)

WHAT IS GOD SAYING TO ME? (Make it personal)

APPLICATION (What will I do?)
- ☐ Step of faith
- ☐ Promise to believe
- ☐ Sin to confess
- ☐ Command to obey
- ☐ Prayer to pray
- ☐ Fear to surrender

TALK IT OVER (Discuss this verse with a friend)

- Who? _____
- When? _____
- Where? _____
- How? _____

"For I am not ashamed of this Good News about Christ. It is the power of God at work, saving everyone who believes" - Romans 1:16

TODAY I AM GRATEFUL FOR:

1.

2.

3.

PRAYER

MEMORY VERSE:

PERSONAL THOUGHTS

_____
_____
_____
_____
_____

DATE: / /20 S M T W T F S

SCRIPTURE (Today's verse)

WHAT IS GOD SAYING TO ME? (Make it personal)

APPLICATION (What will I do?)

□ Step of faith
□ Promise to believe
□ Sin to confess
□ Command to obey
□ Prayer to pray
□ Fear to surrender

TALK IT OVER (Discuss this verse with a friend)

- Who? _____
- When? _____
- Where? _____
- How? _____

"When you place yourself in the hands of Almighty God, EVERYTHING is subject to change." - Paul Brady

TODAY I AM GRATEFUL FOR:

1.

2.

3.

PRAYER

MEMORY VERSE:

PERSONAL THOUGHTS

_____

_____

_____

_____

_____

DATE: / /20 S M T W T F S

SCRIPTURE (Today's verse)

WHAT IS GOD SAYING TO ME? (Make it personal)

APPLICATION (What will I do?)

- ☐ Step of faith
- ☐ Promise to believe
- ☐ Sin to confess
- ☐ Command to obey
- ☐ Prayer to pray
- ☐ Fear to surrender

TALK IT OVER (Discuss this verse with a friend)

- Who? _____
- When? _____
- Where? _____
- How? _____

"Loving God means keeping his commandments, and his commandments are not burdensome." - 1 John 5:3

TODAY I AM GRATEFUL FOR:

1.

2.

3.

PRAYER

MEMORY VERSE:

PERSONAL THOUGHTS

_____

_____

_____

_____

_____

Weekly Review

How did you apply this week's scripture reading?

What steps of faith did you take?

Who did you share Christ with?

What prayers did God answer?

Where do you see growth in your spiritual life?

Next week, with the help of the Holy Spirit:

☐ I will:

☐ I will not:

DATE: / /20   S M T W T F S

SCRIPTURE (Today's verse)

WHAT IS GOD SAYING TO ME? (Make it personal)

APPLICATION (What will I do?)
☐ Step of faith
☐ Promise to believe
☐ Sin to confess
☐ Command to obey
☐ Prayer to pray
☐ Fear to surrender

TALK IT OVER (Discuss this verse with a friend)

- Who?   _____
- When?   _____
- Where?   _____
- How?   _____

"If a church's strategy is not grounded in making disciples, the church has abandoned the mission Christ has given."- Jonathan Hayashi

TODAY I AM GRATEFUL FOR:

1.

2.

3.

PRAYER

MEMORY VERSE:

PERSONAL THOUGHTS

_____

_____

_____

_____

_____

DATE: / /20 S M T W T F S

SCRIPTURE (Today's verse)

WHAT IS GOD SAYING TO ME? (Make it personal)

APPLICATION (What will I do?)
- ☐ Step of faith
- ☐ Promise to believe
- ☐ Sin to confess
- ☐ Command to obey
- ☐ Prayer to pray
- ☐ Fear to surrender

TALK IT OVER (Discuss this verse with a friend)

- Who? _____
- When? _____
- Where? _____
- How? _____

"And all of you, dress yourselves in humility as you relate to one another, for 'God opposes the proud but gives grace to the humble.'" - 1 Peter 5:5

TODAY I AM GRATEFUL FOR:

1.

2.

3.

PRAYER

MEMORY VERSE:

PERSONAL THOUGHTS

_____

_____

_____

_____

_____

DATE: / /20   S M T W T F S

SCRIPTURE (Today's verse)

WHAT IS GOD SAYING TO ME? (Make it personal)

APPLICATION (What will I do?)

☐ Step of faith
☐ Promise to believe
☐ Sin to confess
☐ Command to obey
☐ Prayer to pray
☐ Fear to surrender

TALK IT OVER (Discuss this verse with a friend)

- Who? _____
- When? _____
- Where? _____
- How? _____

144

"The gospel call invites us to apprentice ourselves to Jesus, but few seem willing to sign up as pilgrims in the lifelong adventure of discipleship." - Trevor Hudson

TODAY I AM GRATEFUL FOR:

1.

2.

3.

PRAYER

MEMORY VERSE:

PERSONAL THOUGHTS

_____

_____

_____

_____

_____

DATE: / /20 S M T W T F S

SCRIPTURE (Today's verse)

WHAT IS GOD SAYING TO ME? (Make it personal)

APPLICATION (What will I do?)
- ☐ Step of faith
- ☐ Promise to believe
- ☐ Sin to confess
- ☐ Command to obey
- ☐ Prayer to pray
- ☐ Fear to surrender

TALK IT OVER (Discuss this verse with a friend)

- Who? _____
- When? _____
- Where? _____
- How? _____

"My sheep listen to my voice; I know them, and they follow me." - John 10:27

TODAY I AM GRATEFUL FOR:

1.

2.

3.

PRAYER

MEMORY VERSE:

PERSONAL THOUGHTS

_____

_____

_____

_____

_____

DATE: / /20   S M T W T F S

SCRIPTURE (Today's verse)

WHAT IS GOD SAYING TO ME? (Make it personal)

APPLICATION (What will I do?)
  ☐ Step of faith
  ☐ Promise to believe
  ☐ Sin to confess
  ☐ Command to obey
  ☐ Prayer to pray
  ☐ Fear to surrender

TALK IT OVER (Discuss this verse with a friend)

- Who?   _____
- When?   _____
- Where?   _____
- How?   _____

"Jesus preached discipleship as the greatest opportunity that any human being will ever have." - Dallas Willard

TODAY I AM GRATEFUL FOR:

1.

2.

3.

PRAYER

MEMORY VERSE:

PERSONAL THOUGHTS

_____

_____

_____

_____

_____

DATE: / /20 S M T W T F S

SCRIPTURE (Today's verse)

WHAT IS GOD SAYING TO ME? (Make it personal)

APPLICATION (What will I do?)
- ☐ Step of faith
- ☐ Promise to believe
- ☐ Sin to confess
- ☐ Command to obey
- ☐ Prayer to pray
- ☐ Fear to surrender

TALK IT OVER (Discuss this verse with a friend)

- Who? _____
- When? _____
- Where? _____
- How? _____

"...be strong and immovable. Always work enthusiastically for the Lord, for you know that nothing you do for the Lord is ever useless." - 1 Corinthians 15:58

TODAY I AM GRATEFUL FOR:

1.

2.

3.

PRAYER

MEMORY VERSE:

PERSONAL THOUGHTS

_____

_____

_____

_____

_____

DATE: / /20   S   M   T   W   T   F   S

SCRIPTURE (Today's verse)

WHAT IS GOD SAYING TO ME? (Make it personal)

APPLICATION (What will I do?)
- ☐ Step of faith
- ☐ Promise to believe
- ☐ Sin to confess
- ☐ Command to obey
- ☐ Prayer to pray
- ☐ Fear to surrender

TALK IT OVER (Discuss this verse with a friend)

- Who?   _____
- When?   _____
- Where?   _____
- How?   _____

"Ministering Christ to others so that Jesus might be reproduced and grow in people is the highest service to both God and man." - Henry Hon

TODAY I AM GRATEFUL FOR:

1.

2.

3.

PRAYER

MEMORY VERSE:

PERSONAL THOUGHTS

_____

_____

_____

_____

_____

Weekly Review

How did you apply this week's scripture reading?

What steps of faith did you take?

Who did you share Christ with?

What prayers did God answer?

Where do you see growth in your spiritual life?

Next week, with the help of the Holy Spirit:

□ I will:

□ I will not:

DATE: /   /20   S M T W T F S

SCRIPTURE (Today's verse)

WHAT IS GOD SAYING TO ME? (Make it personal)

APPLICATION (What will I do?)

- ☐ Step of faith
- ☐ Promise to believe
- ☐ Sin to confess
- ☐ Command to obey
- ☐ Prayer to pray
- ☐ Fear to surrender

TALK IT OVER (Discuss this verse with a friend)

- Who?   _____
- When?   _____
- Where?   _____
- How?   _____

"We know what real love is because Jesus gave up his life for us. So we also ought to give up our lives for our brothers and sisters." - 1 John 3:16

TODAY I AM GRATEFUL FOR:

1.

2.

3.

PRAYER

MEMORY VERSE:

PERSONAL THOUGHTS

_____
_____
_____
_____
_____

DATE: /   /20   S   M   T   W   T   F   S

SCRIPTURE (Today's verse)

WHAT IS GOD SAYING TO ME? (Make it personal)

APPLICATION (What will I do?)
- ☐ Step of faith
- ☐ Promise to believe
- ☐ Sin to confess
- ☐ Command to obey
- ☐ Prayer to pray
- ☐ Fear to surrender

TALK IT OVER (Discuss this verse with a friend)

- Who?   _____
- When?   _____
- Where?   _____
- How?   _____

"A true disciple is one who fully serves first the interest of His master by doing nothing of his interest alone but first for his Master's interest . " - Prosper Germoh

TODAY I AM GRATEFUL FOR:

1.

2.

3.

PRAYER

MEMORY VERSE:

PERSONAL THOUGHTS

_____

_____

_____

_____

_____

DATE: / /20   S M T W T F S

SCRIPTURE (Today's verse)

WHAT IS GOD SAYING TO ME? (Make it personal)

APPLICATION (What will I do?)

☐ Step of faith
☐ Promise to believe
☐ Sin to confess
☐ Command to obey
☐ Prayer to pray
☐ Fear to surrender

TALK IT OVER (Discuss this verse with a friend)

- Who?   _____
- When?   _____
- Where?   _____
- How?   _____

160

"Don't copy the behavior and customs of this world, but let God transform you into a new person by changing the way you think." - Romans 12:2

TODAY I AM GRATEFUL FOR:

1.

2.

3.

PRAYER

MEMORY VERSE:

PERSONAL THOUGHTS

_____

_____

_____

_____

_____

DATE: / /20 S M T W T F S

SCRIPTURE (Today's verse)

WHAT IS GOD SAYING TO ME? (Make it personal)

APPLICATION (What will I do?)
- ☐ Step of faith
- ☐ Promise to believe
- ☐ Sin to confess
- ☐ Command to obey
- ☐ Prayer to pray
- ☐ Fear to surrender

TALK IT OVER (Discuss this verse with a friend)

- Who? _____
- When? _____
- Where? _____
- How? _____

162

"Run your race. It's the only one that will count in eternity." - Robin Bertram

TODAY I AM GRATEFUL FOR:

1.

2.

3.

PRAYER

MEMORY VERSE:

PERSONAL THOUGHTS

_____

_____

_____

_____

_____

DATE: / /20 S M T W T F S

SCRIPTURE (Today's verse)

WHAT IS GOD SAYING TO ME? (Make it personal)

APPLICATION (What will I do?)
- ☐ Step of faith
- ☐ Promise to believe
- ☐ Sin to confess
- ☐ Command to obey
- ☐ Prayer to pray
- ☐ Fear to surrender

TALK IT OVER (Discuss this verse with a friend)

- Who?   _____
- When?   _____
- Where?   _____
- How?   _____

"But it is no shame to suffer for being a Christian. Praise God for the privilege of being called by his name!" - 1 Peter 4:16

TODAY I AM GRATEFUL FOR:

1.

2.

3.

PRAYER

MEMORY VERSE:

PERSONAL THOUGHTS

_____

_____

_____

_____

_____

DATE: / /20 S M T W T F S

SCRIPTURE (Today's verse)

WHAT IS GOD SAYING TO ME? (Make it personal)

APPLICATION (What will I do?)

- ☐ Step of faith
- ☐ Promise to believe
- ☐ Sin to confess
- ☐ Command to obey
- ☐ Prayer to pray
- ☐ Fear to surrender

TALK IT OVER (Discuss this verse with a friend)

- Who? _____
- When? _____
- Where? _____
- How? _____

"Good disciplemaking requires both intentionality and relationality. It means being strategic and being social." - David Mathis

TODAY I AM GRATEFUL FOR:

1.

2.

3.

PRAYER

MEMORY VERSE:

PERSONAL THOUGHTS

_____
_____
_____
_____
_____

DATE: / /20 S M T W T F S

SCRIPTURE (Today's verse)

WHAT IS GOD SAYING TO ME? (Make it personal)

APPLICATION (What will I do?)
- ☐ Step of faith
- ☐ Promise to believe
- ☐ Sin to confess
- ☐ Command to obey
- ☐ Prayer to pray
- ☐ Fear to surrender

TALK IT OVER (Discuss this verse with a friend)

- Who? _____
- When? _____
- Where? _____
- How? _____

"Each of you must repent of your sins and turn to God, and be baptized in the name of Jesus Christ for the forgiveness of your sins." - Acts 2:38

TODAY I AM GRATEFUL FOR:

1.

2.

3.

PRAYER

MEMORY VERSE:

PERSONAL THOUGHTS

_____
_____
_____
_____
_____

Weekly Review

How did you apply this week's scripture reading?

What steps of faith did you take?

Who did you share Christ with?

What prayers did God answer?

Where do you see growth in your spiritual life?

Next week, with the help of the Holy Spirit:

☐ I will:

☐ I will not:

DATE: / /20 S M T W T F S

SCRIPTURE (Today's verse)

WHAT IS GOD SAYING TO ME? (Make it personal)

APPLICATION (What will I do?)
- ☐ Step of faith
- ☐ Promise to believe
- ☐ Sin to confess
- ☐ Command to obey
- ☐ Prayer to pray
- ☐ Fear to surrender

TALK IT OVER (Discuss this verse with a friend)

- Who? _____
- When? _____
- Where? _____
- How? _____

172

"If we are not willing to wake up in the morning and die to ourselves, perhaps we should ask ourselves whether or not we are really following Jesus." - Donald Miller

TODAY I AM GRATEFUL FOR:

1.

2.

3.

PRAYER

MEMORY VERSE:

PERSONAL THOUGHTS

_____

_____

_____

_____

_____

DATE: / /20 S M T W T F S

SCRIPTURE (Today's verse)

WHAT IS GOD SAYING TO ME? (Make it personal)

APPLICATION (What will I do?)

☐ Step of faith
☐ Promise to believe
☐ Sin to confess
☐ Command to obey
☐ Prayer to pray
☐ Fear to surrender

TALK IT OVER (Discuss this verse with a friend)

- Who? _____
- When? _____
- Where? _____
- How? _____

174

"You will experience all these blessings if you obey the Lord your God."
- Deuteronomy 28:2

TODAY I AM GRATEFUL FOR:

1.

2.

3.

PRAYER

MEMORY VERSE:

PERSONAL THOUGHTS

DATE: /   /20   S   M   T   W   T   F   S

SCRIPTURE (Today's verse)

WHAT IS GOD SAYING TO ME? (Make it personal)

APPLICATION (What will I do?)
- ☐   Step of faith
- ☐   Promise to believe
- ☐   Sin to confess
- ☐   Command to obey
- ☐   Prayer to pray
- ☐   Fear to surrender

TALK IT OVER (Discuss this verse with a friend)

- Who?   _____
- When?   _____
- Where?   _____
- How?   _____

"Holiness does not consist in doing extraordinary things. It consists in accepting and following the will of God." - Mother Theresa

TODAY I AM GRATEFUL FOR:

1.

2.

3.

PRAYER

MEMORY VERSE:

PERSONAL THOUGHTS

_____
_____
_____
_____
_____

DATE: / /20 S M T W T F S

SCRIPTURE (Today's verse)

WHAT IS GOD SAYING TO ME? (Make it personal)

APPLICATION (What will I do?)
- ☐ Step of faith
- ☐ Promise to believe
- ☐ Sin to confess
- ☐ Command to obey
- ☐ Prayer to pray
- ☐ Fear to surrender

TALK IT OVER (Discuss this verse with a friend)

- Who? _____
- When? _____
- Where? _____
- How? _____

"He saved us, not because of the righteous things we had done, but because of his mercy." - Titus 3:5

TODAY I AM GRATEFUL FOR:

1.

2.

3.

PRAYER

MEMORY VERSE:

PERSONAL THOUGHTS

_____

_____

_____

_____

_____

DATE: / /20   S M T W T F S

SCRIPTURE (Today's verse)

WHAT IS GOD SAYING TO ME? (Make it personal)

APPLICATION (What will I do?)
- ☐ Step of faith
- ☐ Promise to believe
- ☐ Sin to confess
- ☐ Command to obey
- ☐ Prayer to pray
- ☐ Fear to surrender

TALK IT OVER (Discuss this verse with a friend)

- Who?   _____
- When?   _____
- Where?   _____
- How?   _____

"Don't follow a defeated foe. Follow Christ. It is costly. You will be an exile in this age. But you will be free." - John Piper

TODAY I AM GRATEFUL FOR:

1.

2.

3.

PRAYER

MEMORY VERSE:

PERSONAL THOUGHTS

_____

_____

_____

_____

_____

DATE: /   /20   S   M   T   W   T   F   S

SCRIPTURE (Today's verse)

WHAT IS GOD SAYING TO ME? (Make it personal)

APPLICATION (What will I do?)

- ☐ Step of faith
- ☐ Promise to believe
- ☐ Sin to confess
- ☐ Command to obey
- ☐ Prayer to pray
- ☐ Fear to surrender

TALK IT OVER (Discuss this verse with a friend)

- Who?   _____
- When?   _____
- Where?   _____
- How?   _____

"Those who say they live in God should live their lives as Jesus did." - 1 John 2:6

TODAY I AM GRATEFUL FOR:

1.

2.

3.

PRAYER

MEMORY VERSE:

PERSONAL THOUGHTS

_____

_____

_____

_____

_____

DATE: / /20 S M T W T F S

SCRIPTURE (Today's verse)

WHAT IS GOD SAYING TO ME? (Make it personal)

APPLICATION (What will I do?)

☐ Step of faith
☐ Promise to believe
☐ Sin to confess
☐ Command to obey
☐ Prayer to pray
☐ Fear to surrender

TALK IT OVER (Discuss this verse with a friend)

- Who? _____
- When? _____
- Where? _____
- How? _____

184

"All suffering is worth it to follow Jesus. He is that amazing." - Nabeel Qureshi

TODAY I AM GRATEFUL FOR:

1.

2.

3.

PRAYER

MEMORY VERSE:

PERSONAL THOUGHTS

_____
_____
_____
_____
_____

Weekly Review

How did you apply this week's scripture reading?

What steps of faith did you take?

Who did you share Christ with?

What prayers did God answer?

Where do you see growth in your spiritual life?

Next week, with the help of the Holy Spirit:

☐ I will:

☐ I will not:

DATE: / /20 S M T W T F S

SCRIPTURE (Today's verse)

WHAT IS GOD SAYING TO ME? (Make it personal)

APPLICATION (What will I do?)

- ☐ Step of faith
- ☐ Promise to believe
- ☐ Sin to confess
- ☐ Command to obey
- ☐ Prayer to pray
- ☐ Fear to surrender

TALK IT OVER (Discuss this verse with a friend)

- Who? _____
- When? _____
- Where? _____
- How? _____

"Those who love their life in this world will lose it. Those who care nothing for their life in this world will keep it for eternity." - John 12:25

TODAY I AM GRATEFUL FOR:

1.

2.

3.

PRAYER

MEMORY VERSE:

PERSONAL THOUGHTS

_____

_____

_____

_____

_____

DATE: / /20 S M T W T F S

SCRIPTURE (Today's verse)

WHAT IS GOD SAYING TO ME? (Make it personal)

APPLICATION (What will I do?)

☐ Step of faith
☐ Promise to believe
☐ Sin to confess
☐ Command to obey
☐ Prayer to pray
☐ Fear to surrender

TALK IT OVER (Discuss this verse with a friend)

- Who?   _____
- When?   _____
- Where?   _____
- How?   _____

"Following Jesus isn't something you can do at night where no one notices. It's a twenty-four-hour-a-day commitment that will interfere with your life." - Kyle Idleman

TODAY I AM GRATEFUL FOR:

1.

2.

3.

PRAYER

MEMORY VERSE:

PERSONAL THOUGHTS

_____

_____

_____

_____

_____

DATE: / /20   S M T W T F S

SCRIPTURE (Today's verse)

WHAT IS GOD SAYING TO ME? (Make it personal)

APPLICATION (What will I do?)
- ☐ Step of faith
- ☐ Promise to believe
- ☐ Sin to confess
- ☐ Command to obey
- ☐ Prayer to pray
- ☐ Fear to surrender

TALK IT OVER (Discuss this verse with a friend)

- Who?   _____
- When?   _____
- Where?   _____
- How?   _____

"This means that God's holy people must endure persecution patiently, obeying his commands and maintaining their faith in Jesus." - Revelation 14:12

TODAY I AM GRATEFUL FOR:

1.

2.

3.

PRAYER

MEMORY VERSE:

PERSONAL THOUGHTS

_____
_____
_____
_____
_____

DATE: / /20   S M T W T F S

SCRIPTURE (Today's verse)

WHAT IS GOD SAYING TO ME? (Make it personal)

APPLICATION (What will I do?)
- ☐ Step of faith
- ☐ Promise to believe
- ☐ Sin to confess
- ☐ Command to obey
- ☐ Prayer to pray
- ☐ Fear to surrender

TALK IT OVER (Discuss this verse with a friend)

- Who?   _____
- When?   _____
- Where?   _____
- How?   _____

"Instant obedience will teach you more about God than a lifetime of Bible discussions. "
- Rick Warren

TODAY I AM GRATEFUL FOR:

1.

2.

3.

PRAYER

MEMORY VERSE:

PERSONAL THOUGHTS

DATE: /   /20   S M T W T F S

SCRIPTURE (Today's verse)

WHAT IS GOD SAYING TO ME? (Make it personal)

APPLICATION (What will I do?)
- ☐ Step of faith
- ☐ Promise to believe
- ☐ Sin to confess
- ☐ Command to obey
- ☐ Prayer to pray
- ☐ Fear to surrender

TALK IT OVER (Discuss this verse with a friend)

- Who?   _____
- When?   _____
- Where?   _____
- How?   _____

"For this is how God loved the world: He gave his one and only Son, so that everyone who believes in him will not perish but have eternal life." - John 3:16

TODAY I AM GRATEFUL FOR:

1.

2.

3.

PRAYER

MEMORY VERSE:

PERSONAL THOUGHTS

_____

_____

_____

_____

_____

DATE: / /20 S M T W T F S

SCRIPTURE (Today's verse)

WHAT IS GOD SAYING TO ME? (Make it personal)

APPLICATION (What will I do?)
- ☐ Step of faith
- ☐ Promise to believe
- ☐ Sin to confess
- ☐ Command to obey
- ☐ Prayer to pray
- ☐ Fear to surrender

TALK IT OVER (Discuss this verse with a friend)

- Who? _____
- When? _____
- Where? _____
- How? _____

"Obedience unites us so closely to God that it in a way transforms us into Him, so that we have no other will but His." - Thomas Aquinas

TODAY I AM GRATEFUL FOR:

1.

2.

3.

PRAYER

MEMORY VERSE:

PERSONAL THOUGHTS

_____

_____

_____

_____

_____

DATE: /   /20   S   M   T   W   T   F   S

SCRIPTURE (Today's verse)

WHAT IS GOD SAYING TO ME? (Make it personal)

APPLICATION (What will I do?)
- ☐ Step of faith
- ☐ Promise to believe
- ☐ Sin to confess
- ☐ Command to obey
- ☐ Prayer to pray
- ☐ Fear to surrender

TALK IT OVER (Discuss this verse with a friend)

- Who?   _____
- When?   _____
- Where?   _____
- How?   _____

"You must love the Lord your God with all your heart, all your soul, all your strength, and all your mind.' And, 'Love your neighbor as yourself." - Luke 10:27

TODAY I AM GRATEFUL FOR:

1.

2.

3.

PRAYER

MEMORY VERSE:

PERSONAL THOUGHTS

_____

_____

_____

_____

_____

Weekly Review

How did you apply this week's scripture reading?

What steps of faith did you take?

Who did you share Christ with?

What prayers did God answer?

Where do you see growth in your spiritual life?

Next week, with the help of the Holy Spirit:

☐   I will:

☐   I will not:

DATE: /   /20   S   M   T   W   T   F   S

SCRIPTURE (Today's verse)

WHAT IS GOD SAYING TO ME? (Make it personal)

APPLICATION (What will I do?)
- ☐ Step of faith
- ☐ Promise to believe
- ☐ Sin to confess
- ☐ Command to obey
- ☐ Prayer to pray
- ☐ Fear to surrender

TALK IT OVER (Discuss this verse with a friend)

- Who?   _____
- When?   _____
- Where?   _____
- How?   _____

"God doesn't want our success; He wants us. He doesn't demand our achievements; He demands our obedience." - Charles W. Colson

TODAY I AM GRATEFUL FOR:

1.

2.

3.

PRAYER

MEMORY VERSE:

PERSONAL THOUGHTS

_____
_____
_____
_____
_____

DATE: / /20 S M T W T F S

SCRIPTURE (Today's verse)

WHAT IS GOD SAYING TO ME? (Make it personal)

APPLICATION (What will I do?)
- ☐ Step of faith
- ☐ Promise to believe
- ☐ Sin to confess
- ☐ Command to obey
- ☐ Prayer to pray
- ☐ Fear to surrender

TALK IT OVER (Discuss this verse with a friend)

- Who? _____
- When? _____
- Where? _____
- How? _____

"But the Holy Spirit produces this kind of fruit in our lives: love, joy, peace, patience, kindness, goodness, faithfulness, gentleness, and self-control." Galatians 5:22-23

TODAY I AM GRATEFUL FOR:

1.

2.

3.

PRAYER

MEMORY VERSE:

PERSONAL THOUGHTS

_____

_____

_____

_____

_____

DATE: /   /20   S   M   T   W   T   F   S

SCRIPTURE (Today's verse)

WHAT IS GOD SAYING TO ME? (Make it personal)

APPLICATION (What will I do?)
- ☐ Step of faith
- ☐ Promise to believe
- ☐ Sin to confess
- ☐ Command to obey
- ☐ Prayer to pray
- ☐ Fear to surrender

TALK IT OVER (Discuss this verse with a friend)

- Who?   _____
- When?   _____
- Where?   _____
- How?   _____

TODAY I AM GRATEFUL FOR:

1.

2.

3.

PRAYER

MEMORY VERSE:

PERSONAL THOUGHTS

_____

_____

_____

_____

_____

DATE: / /20   S   M   T   W   T   F   S

SCRIPTURE (Today's verse)

WHAT IS GOD SAYING TO ME? (Make it personal)

APPLICATION (What will I do?)
- ☐ Step of faith
- ☐ Promise to believe
- ☐ Sin to confess
- ☐ Command to obey
- ☐ Prayer to pray
- ☐ Fear to surrender

TALK IT OVER (Discuss this verse with a friend)

- Who?   _____
- When?   _____
- Where?   _____
- How?   _____

"Yes, I am the vine; you are the branches. Those who remain in me, and I in them, will produce much fruit. For apart from me you can do nothing." - John 15:5

TODAY I AM GRATEFUL FOR:

1.

2.

3.

PRAYER

MEMORY VERSE:

PERSONAL THOUGHTS

_____

_____

_____

_____

_____

DATE: /   /20   S   M   T   W   T   F   S

SCRIPTURE (Today's verse)

WHAT IS GOD SAYING TO ME? (Make it personal)

APPLICATION (What will I do?)
- ☐ Step of faith
- ☐ Promise to believe
- ☐ Sin to confess
- ☐ Command to obey
- ☐ Prayer to pray
- ☐ Fear to surrender

TALK IT OVER (Discuss this verse with a friend)

- Who?   _____
- When?   _____
- Where?   _____
- How?   _____

212

"He is no fool who gives what he cannot keep to gain that which he cannot lose."
- Jim Elliott

TODAY I AM GRATEFUL FOR:

1.

2.

3.

PRAYER

MEMORY VERSE:

PERSONAL THOUGHTS

_____

_____

_____

_____

_____

213

DATE: / /20 S M T W T F S

SCRIPTURE (Today's verse)

WHAT IS GOD SAYING TO ME? (Make it personal)

APPLICATION (What will I do?)
- ☐ Step of faith
- ☐ Promise to believe
- ☐ Sin to confess
- ☐ Command to obey
- ☐ Prayer to pray
- ☐ Fear to surrender

TALK IT OVER (Discuss this verse with a friend)

- Who?   _____
- When?   _____
- Where?   _____
- How?   _____

"So you see, faith by itself isn't enough. Unless it produces good deeds, it is dead and useless." - James 2:17

TODAY I AM GRATEFUL FOR:

1.

2.

3.

PRAYER

MEMORY VERSE:

PERSONAL THOUGHTS

_____

_____

_____

_____

_____

Final Thoughts

Congratulations on 90 days of spiritual growth. I am incredibly proud of you!

As you reflect over this past three months, you have read God's Word, you heard the voice of the Holy Spirit, and you took action to obey what you learned. You also committed the process to God in prayer and found accountability by sharing with a friend.

It is my prayer that you have found consistency in your time with God, and I trust that you are experiencing a deeper, more intimate relationship with Jesus.

The discipleship journey does not stop here. I hope you will pick up another copy of this journal and begin your next 90 days.

As you move forward in your relationship with God, be looking for the next steps, God is asking you to take. Until we meet Jesus face to face, our journey does not stop.

Discipleship is about continually taking the next steps. To be a follower of Jesus, you have to follow. So many Christians move forward until they find a place of comfort in their faith. It's here that, tragically, they plateau in their faith and stop growing. This is not God's plan, nor his will.

"The righteous keep moving forward, and those with clean hands become stronger and stronger." (Job 17:9 NLT)

It is God's will for us to keep growing in our knowledge of Jesus and continually be transformed to be like Christ.

Thank you for joining me on this journey!

Loren Hicks
5minutediscipleship.com

Keep the Conversation Going

If you would like to join an encouraging and inspiring community of disciples of Jesus, please join the free 5 Minute Discipleship Facebook group:

5minutedisicpleship.com/fb

Do You Recommend This Journal?

If you liked this journal, it would mean so much if you would take a moment and leave an honest review on Amazon. Thank you very much!

About the Author

Loren Hicks is a pastor who is passionate about helping people become fully devoted followers of Jesus. Previously he served as a University Campus pastor and a church leadership consultant. He and his wife Linda live on the Central Coast of California. Together they have three daughters.

Loren is also the host of The 5 Minute Discipleship Podcast. Every day he shares short episodes that are easy to follow and apply to your life. You can listen on Apple Podcasts and all the major podcast platforms.

Want to know more?

Check out his blog and podcast at 5minutediscipleship.com. You can follow on Facebook and Instagram @5minutediscipleship.

If you have a story of how this journal has helped you grow as a follower of Jesus, he would love to hear from you. You can email him at loren@5minutediscipleship.com.